The Pocket Guide to Practice Value Creation

Growing Your Medical Practice without Burning Out

By

Theo Harvey, M.S, MBA

The Pocket Guide to Practice Value Creation

Growing Your Medical Practice without Burning Out

Contents

Embracing Change in Healthcare

As a healthcare professional, you understand the constant undercurrent of change in your industry more intimately than most. The landscape of healthcare has always been dynamic, yet the pace of transformation in recent years has been unprecedented. For doctors, nurse practitioners, and medical practice owners, staying abreast of these changes isn't just about adapting—it's about seizing opportunities to improve, grow, and redefine what success looks like in your practices. The journey of embracing change in healthcare can be as rewarding as it is essential.

It's easy to view change as a force to be managed or, at times, battled. However, by shifting your mindset to see change as an ally, you can unlock the potential to not only survive but thrive. This book is dedicated to helping you navigate the ever-evolving healthcare environment with actionable steps to grow your business. Through a blend of persuasive narratives, instructional advice, and motivational stories, we'll explore how embracing change can lead to significant growth and transformation in your medical practice.

The essence of growth in healthcare lies in understanding the importance of patient-centric services, integrating innovative technologies, and fostering a culture of continuous improvement and collaboration. By laying the foundation for growth, overcoming revenue losses, enhancing patient satisfaction, building high-performance teams, leveraging healthcare innovations, and achieving financial and operational excellence, medical practices can position themselves as leaders in the new healthcare era.

Each chapter of this book serves as a guidepost on your journey through the changes shaping our industry. From overcoming the fears associated with change to recognizing the trajectories that innovation and collaboration can unlock, our discussion will empower you to take bold steps forward. We're not just talking about growth in numbers, but growth in quality, impact, and fulfillment. It's about creating a legacy of excellence, compassion, and resilience in healthcare.

In embracing change, we do so with the understanding that the heart of healthcare remains unchanged: your commitment to the well-being of your patients. Let this book be your compass as you navigate the twists and turns of the industry, armed with the knowledge, strategies, and mindset needed to flourish. Together, let's step forward into this new chapter of healthcare, embracing change not just as a challenge, but as an opportunity to redefine what's possible in your practice and for your patients.

Chapter 1:
Laying the Foundation for Growth

In the ever-evolving world of healthcare, positioning your medical practice for growth requires both vision and foundation. This chapter embarks upon the critical journey of recalibrating your mindset, establishing the groundwork for an expansive future. Here, we delve into why this moment presents a unique opportunity for growth. Amidst advancements in healthcare technology, shifting patient expectations, and dynamic regulatory landscapes, your practice's potential to flourish has never been more tangible. Understanding your current practice landscape is equally pivotal. It's about comprehensively assessing where you stand today—your strengths, areas for improvement, patient demographics, and the competitive ecosystem. This isn't about quick wins but setting a strategic base, fostering an environment ripe for innovation, efficiency, and enhanced patient care. With the right foundation, your practice isn't just surviving; it's primed to thrive, adapt, and lead in the healthcare journey ahead. Let's embark on this path together, embracing the changes and challenges, with the cornerstone of growth firmly in hand. By invoking a blend of introspection and forward-thinking, we lay the scaffolding for a practice that not only grows but becomes a beacon of excellence and patient-centric care in the healthcare industry.

Why Now Is the Perfect Time to Grow Your Medical Practice

In the rapidly evolving world of healthcare, standing still is not an option. The digital age has ushered in a period of unprecedented change, challenging medical practices to adapt or risk being left behind. More specifically, the recent pandemic has fundamentally changed how you practice medicine. Yet, with challenge comes opportunity. This moment, right now, presents a golden opportunity to steer your practice toward growth and improved patient care. Whether you're a seasoned doctor, an enthusiastic nurse practitioner, or a motivated medical practice owner, this call to action is for you. Let's explore why the timing couldn't be more perfect.

The landscape of healthcare is shifting, thanks in part to technological advances and changing patient expectations. Today's patients are more informed and more involved in their healthcare decisions than ever before. They demand convenience, transparency, and personalization. This shift has opened the door for practices willing to innovate and align with these evolving expectations. It's not just about offering care; it's about offering care that's accessible, patient-centric, and technologically adept.

Moreover, the advent of telehealth has broken down traditional barriers to care, extending the reach of your practice beyond its physical walls. Enlightened by the convenience it offers, many patients now prefer telehealth options for non-emergency consultations. This isn't just a temporary shift; it's a marker of the future, a future where your practice can serve a broader community, enhancing both growth and impact.

Additionally, the current healthcare ecosystem is ripe for practices that prioritize operational efficiency and patient satisfaction. Regulations and reimbursements are increasingly tied to patient outcomes and experiences. By focusing on these areas, you're not just investing in growth; you're aligning with the direction of healthcare itself. Practices that can navigate these regulations effectively will find themselves ahead, both financially and in the quality of care provided.

There's also a growing acknowledgment within the healthcare community about the importance of mental health. As stigma fades, demand for mental health services is rising. This presents an opportune moment for practices to expand their services to include mental health care, tapping into a growing need and demonstrating a commitment to comprehensive patient care.

Financial incentives are another reason for optimism. With various government and private programs offering incentives for innovation, quality care, and efficiency, there's never been a better time to invest in your practice's growth. These incentives are designed to support practices in their journey toward improved patient care and operational excellence. They provide a financial cushion that can help mitigate the risks associated with growth and investment.

It's also worth noting that the competition is no longer just the practice next door. Healthcare is globalizing, and patients often review their options on a much broader scale. However, this also means your potential patient base is expanding. By focusing on specialized services or exceptional patient care, you can attract patients from a wider geographic area, tapping into markets previously beyond reach.

Let's not forget, growth is not just about expansion; it's about evolution. It's a process of continually improving your practice to meet the changing needs of healthcare and your patients. This aspect of growth ensures your practice remains relevant, resilient, and ready for the challenges of tomorrow.

The keys to unlocking this growth lie within your grasp. By embracing innovation, focusing on patient experience, and leveraging the available financial incentives, you can set your practice on a path to sustainable growth. It's a journey that will require dedication, flexibility, and a willingness to step out of comfort zones. Yet, the rewards — a thriving practice, satisfied patients, and a fulfilling career — are well worth the effort.

In closing, the perfect time to grow your medical practice is now. It's an era of change, challenge, and tremendous opportunity. As we move forward into the chapters ahead, we'll explore actionable steps to capitalize on these opportunities, laying a strong foundation for the sustainable growth of your practice. The path to growth is clear, and the first step on that path is deciding to embark on the journey. Let's make today the day you choose to take that step.

Understanding Your Current Practice Landscape

As we delve into the crucial step of understanding your current practice landscape, it's essential to adopt a stance of both introspection and forward-thinking. Imagine standing on a precipice with a powerful telescope; your medical practice is behind you, and ahead is the vast, uncharted territory of potential growth. This analogy isn't merely poetic—it's a call to action. Recognizing where you currently stand, in terms of operational efficiency, patient satisfaction, team dynamics, and financial health, sets the stage for impactful growth strategies.

Firstly, conduct a thorough assessment of your practice's operational workflow. How seamless are your administrative processes? Are there bottlenecks that consistently slow down productivity or patient flow? It's akin to diagnosing a patient; identifying these operational symptoms early, allows for a more effective treatment plan—streamlining processes and eliminating inefficiencies. Moreover, this assessment should extend to your team's dynamics. A high-performing team is the heartbeat of any successful practice. Reflect on your current culture, communication channels, and the alignment of team members with your practice's core values and goals. Is there congruence, or are there discrepancies that need addressing?

Additionally, understanding your financial standing is not just about knowing your current revenue streams. It's about comprehensively analyzing the profitability of different services, patient demographics that drive the most revenue, and areas where resources may be leaking or underutilized. This financial audit is critical, as it guides where to focus growth initiatives for the highest return on investment. Engaging in this detailed financial introspection will illuminate paths to enhanced profitability that may have previously been overshadowed by day-to-day operations.

Equally important is gauging patient satisfaction and engagement. In the modern healthcare landscape, the patient experience is paramount. How do your patients feel about their interactions with your practice? Are there services they desire that you're not offering? Feedback from patients can be a goldmine of information, revealing both strengths to build upon and weaknesses to address. Remember, a satisfied patient is not just a repeat client, but also a potential ambassador for your practice in the community.

Finally, take stock of how well your practice is integrating and leveraging technology. The right technological tools can significantly elevate your practice's efficiency, patient satisfaction, and even team morale. Are you using the most up-to-date and efficient software for billing, scheduling, and patient records? Is there a technology gap that if bridged, could propel your practice forward? In the swiftly evolving field of healthcare, staying abreast of technological advancements is not optional; it's imperative for growth.

In sum, understanding your current practice landscape is a comprehensive exercise that spans operational, financial, team, patient satisfaction, and technological dimensions. Each of these facets offers unique insights into how your practice can not only survive but thrive. By conducting this in-depth analysis, you're laying the groundwork for strategic decisions that will catalyze your practice's growth in meaningful, sustainable ways. It's an initial step that's both reflective and forward-looking—an essential balance for any practice poised for growth.

Chapter 2: Identifying and Overcoming Revenue Loss

In the quest to turn a medical practice into a flourishing enterprise, understanding and addressing the root causes of revenue loss is a pivotal step. When we peel back the layers, it's clear that revenue isn't just slipping through overt gaps like claim denials or late payments; it's also quietly eroding due to inefficiencies and overlooked aspects of practice management. The journey to a more prosperous practice requires a keen eye—to spot the nuanced ways money might be leaving the table—and a strategic mind to implement solutions that not only plug these leaks but also pave the way for enhanced revenue generation. It's about transforming challenges into opportunities for growth. This chapter doesn't just aim to highlight the usual suspects behind revenue loss; instead, it delves deeper, uncovering the hidden factors that are often overlooked. From there, we'll navigate through actionable strategies to reduce administrative burdens that, while seemingly mundane, can have a profound impact on your bottom line. It's crucial to remember that every dollar saved from these leaks is a dollar that can be reinvested into your practice, driving innovation, patient satisfaction, and ultimately, growth. With a blend of resilience, innovation, and strategic action, overcoming revenue loss is not just a possibility; it's a stepping stone to elevate your medical practice to new heights of success and sustainability.

The Hidden Factors That Contribute to Medical Practice Revenue Loss

In the journey toward a flourishing medical practice, understanding and addressing the subtleties that nibble away at your revenue is essential. Often, these factors are not immediately apparent, lurking beneath the surface of day-to-day operations. Identifying these hidden factors is the first crucial step towards reinvigorating your practice's financial health and setting the stage for sustainable growth. This section delves into the oft-overlooked aspects that can lead to surprising drains on your practice's revenue.

Firstly, one of the most underestimated aspects is the cost of poor patient scheduling and no-shows. Every empty slot in your schedule is a missed opportunity for revenue. However, it's not just about missed appointments; inefficient scheduling that doesn't optimize the flow of patients can lead to reduced patient numbers over the course of a day, thereby diminishing your practice's earning potential. Optimizing your scheduling system, perhaps through automated reminders or a more dynamic booking process, can significantly plug this inadvertent leak in your practice's revenue stream.

Secondly, underutilized staff talents and capabilities can lead to indirect revenue loss. Your team's skills and their deployment within your practice don't always align perfectly. In some instances, highly skilled professionals spend an inordinate amount of time on administrative tasks that could be automated or assigned to less specialized staff. This misallocation not only dampens morale but also leads to a drop in productivity and, by extension, revenue. Ensuring that every team member works at the top of their license and leverages their unique strengths can enhance efficiency and patient care, leading to improved revenue.

Furthermore, inadequate coding practices and failure to stay updated with billing regulations can result in denied claims or underpayments. The landscape of medical billing is fraught with complexities and continuous changes. Without a robust process to capture all billable services accurately and stay abreast of current coding standards, you're likely leaving money on the table. Investing in ongoing education for your coding team or considering outsourced expertise could rectify this issue, ensuring you're fully compensated for the services provided.

Lastly, neglecting the power of patient engagement and satisfaction can subtly erode your practice's earnings. In a world where patients have options and voice their opinions widely, a practice that fails to prioritize the patient experience might see a slow but steady decrease in patient retention and referral rates. Cultivating a practice environment that values feedback, fosters communication, and prioritizes patient comfort can transform patient satisfaction into a formidable asset for your practice's growth and financial well-being.

In essence, addressing these hidden factors requires a shift in perspective, seeing beyond the immediate concerns of day-to-day operations to recognize the undercurrents that affect your practice's revenue. With a proactive approach and strategic adjustments, you can uncover these hidden leaks and steer your practice towards a future marked by growth and financial resilience.

Reducing Administrative Burdens

At the heart of a thriving medical practice lies an efficient, streamlined operation that empowers healthcare providers to focus on what they do best: delivering top-quality patient care. One significant obstacle to this efficiency, however, stems from the weight of administrative burdens that can drag down productivity and erode revenue. But fear not, as there are actionable steps you can take to lighten this load and steer your practice towards more fertile grounds for growth.

The first step in reducing administrative hurdles is to take a comprehensive audit of your current processes. Determine where bottlenecks are occurring, whether in patient intake, billing, or appointment scheduling. Understanding these pain points is critical as it forms the basis for implementing changes that can have immediate impacts on your practice's operational efficiency. Remember, you can't fix what you don't know is broken, so this audit is an indispensable part of the process.

Once you've identified the areas that need improvement, consider adopting more advanced technological solutions. Today's medical practices are fortunate to have access to a plethora of software tools designed to streamline just about every administrative task, from electronic health records (EHR) systems that simplify patient data management to automated billing platforms that ensure accuracy and reduce time spent on manual input. Investing in the right technology not only improves efficiency but also significantly cuts down on the potential for human error, a win-win for both your practice and your patients.

Delegation is another powerful strategy in the fight against administrative bloat. Often, highly skilled professionals in the medical field spend far too much time on tasks that don't require their level of expertise. By training and empowering your staff to take on more of these administrative responsibilities, you free up your medical professionals to concentrate on patient care. This not only boosts morale by ensuring that everyone is working to their strengths but also increases the number of patients you can see and effectively treat.

Another often overlooked aspect of reducing administrative burdens is the optimization of patient flow within your practice. Patient scheduling and throughput are areas ripe for improvement in many practices. Implementing strategies like staggered scheduling or telehealth options can minimize wait times and improve the overall patient experience, leading to higher satisfaction and retention rates. This optimization doesn't just make for happier patients; it makes for a more efficient practice that can see more patients without sacrificing the quality of care.

Communication, both internal and external, is key to reducing administrative burdens. Clear, consistent communication strategies can alleviate misunderstandings, prevent errors, and ensure that your practice runs smoothly. Utilizing secure messaging apps and patient portals not only facilitates better communication with patients but also helps in maintaining a cohesive team dynamic among your staff, contributing to a more efficient and less stressful workspace.

Don't forget about the power of training. Investing in regular, comprehensive training sessions for your team can drastically reduce the time and resources spent on correcting mistakes. A well-trained staff is more autonomous, confident, and capable of handling complex administrative tasks, further lightening the load on your healthcare providers and contributing to the overall efficiency and effectiveness of your practice.

In this journey to reduce administrative burdens, it's also vital to maintain a culture of continuous improvement. Encourage feedback from your team and patients about the changes you implement. This feedback is gold dust—it helps you tweak your processes and policies to better meet the needs of those you serve. Remember, streamlining your practice's operations is not a one-time task but an ongoing endeavor.

Additionally, consider periodically revisiting your audit and the strategies you've implemented. The healthcare landscape is ever-changing, and a process or tool that worked wonders yesterday might not be as effective today. Staying agile and open to change ensures that your practice can adapt and thrive, regardless of the challenges that come your way.

Reducing the administrative burdens within your medical practice is not just about improving the bottom line—it's about reclaiming the time and energy that can be better spent on providing excellent patient care, fostering innovation, and supporting your team's professional growth. By taking decisive steps towards streamlining your operations, you're laying down the foundation for a practice that is not only more profitable but also more fulfilling for everyone involved. It's a journey worth embarking on, for the sake of your team, your patients, and the wider community you serve.

Chapter 3:
Enhancing Patient Satisfaction and Engagement

As we navigate the evolving landscape of healthcare, it's clear that the heartbeat of growth lies in the very essence of medical practice: the patients. Fostering an environment where patient satisfaction and engagement are not merely byproducts, but rather integral goals, is essential. The essence of this chapter is to demystify how we can elevate the patient experience to not only meet but surpass expectations. It's about transforming the patient's journey into one that's as seamless and personalized as the care we aspire to provide. By integrating remote communication tactics, we can keep the lines open, making patients feel heard and valued even outside the clinical setting. Moreover, adopting a patient-first approach amplifies this effect, enabling patients to actively participate in their healthcare decisions and feel truly seen.

Enhancing patient satisfaction isn't just about adding value to their experience; it's about reimagining our roles as facilitators of health and wellbeing. This chapter dives deep into actionable strategies that put the patient at the forefront, ensuring that every interaction is an opportunity to build trust and deepen engagement. After all, satisfied and engaged patients are more likely to adhere to treatment plans, return for follow-up care, and advocate for your practice through word of mouth. In essence, by prioritizing patient satisfaction, we not only cultivate a loyal patient base but also stride towards a more sustainable and thriving practice. Let's embark on this journey together, embracing each opportunity to enhance patient satisfaction and engagement as a stepping stone towards unprecedented growth.

Keep Patient Satisfaction High with Remote Communication

In the ever-evolving landscape of healthcare, where convenience and efficiency are increasingly becoming the cornerstone of patient satisfaction, remote communication stands out as a beacon of progress. As medical practices strive towards enhancing patient satisfaction and engagement, mastering the art of remote communication is no longer optional—it's essential. Let's explore actionable steps to leverage this powerful tool, transforming the way we connect with and care for our patients.

The advent of technology in healthcare has ushered in a new era where distance no longer dictates the quality of patient care. Telehealth and other forms of remote communication have broken down geographical barriers, offering patients access to their healthcare providers with unprecedented ease. To make the most of this, practices must ensure that their remote communication channels—be it video calls, emails, or messaging platforms—are as seamless and user-friendly as possible. This begins with choosing the right technology platforms that prioritize security and simplicity.

But it's not just about the technology. At its heart, effective remote communication is about nurturing relationships. It's about making each patient feel heard, understood, and valued, even through a screen. This means being mindful of communication tone, maintaining eye contact during video calls, and being fully present. Patients who feel a personal connection with their healthcare providers are more likely to report higher satisfaction levels, adhere to treatment plans, and engage in proactive health management.

Training your team is critical to achieving this. Equip your staff with the tools and knowledge they need to communicate effectively in a remote setting. This includes technical training on the platforms being used, as well as soft skills training to enhance empathy, active listening, and patient education techniques. Remember, the efficiency of your team in managing remote communications can significantly impact patient satisfaction.

Another key aspect is accessibility. Ensure that your remote communication channels are accessible to all patients, including those with disabilities or those who may not be technologically savvy. This might involve providing instructions in multiple languages, offering technical support, and ensuring that digital platforms are compliant with regulations for accessibility.

Feedback loops are invaluable. Actively seek out and encourage feedback from your patients regarding their remote communication experiences. This will not only provide insights into areas for improvement but also make your patients feel involved in the process of enhancing the quality of care they receive. Implementing changes based on patient feedback can lead to improvements in service delivery and patient satisfaction.

The integration of remote communication should also be seen as an opportunity to reinforce your practice's commitment to patient-centric care. Personalizing communication, respecting patient preferences, and ensuring continuity of care are all facilitated by effective use of remote communication tools. When patients know that their healthcare providers are just a message or call away, it enhances trust and fosters a stronger provider-patient relationship.

Moreover, proactive communication is key. Don't just wait for your patients to reach out with concerns or questions. Use remote communication tools to send out reminders for appointments, follow-ups after consultations, and educational content that empowers patients to take charge of their health. This proactive approach not only improves patient engagement but also demonstrates your practice's commitment to their overall well-being.

In conclusion, remote communication is a powerful tool in the arsenal of modern medical practices aimed at enhancing patient satisfaction and engagement. It's about much more than just digitizing patient interactions; it's about redefining the patient-care provider relationship in a way that is more inclusive, accessible, and supportive than ever before. By focusing on technology, training, accessibility, feedback, personalization, and proactive communication, medical practices can ensure that their journey towards enhanced patient satisfaction is both successful and sustainable.

As we forge ahead, embracing the potential of remote communication will not only keep patient satisfaction high but will also position your practice as a forward-thinking, patient-first healthcare provider. The future of healthcare is here, and it is deeply interconnected with how effectively we can communicate and care for our patients, regardless of distance.

Implementing a Patient-First Approach

In the ever-evolving landscape of healthcare, where the balance between providing exemplary patient care and managing a successful practice is increasingly challenging, a patient-first approach emerges not just as a noble pursuit but as a strategic imperative. This perspective urges us to flip the script, placing the patient's needs, preferences, and values at the forefront of every decision and action. It's about seeing beyond the medical charts and recognizing the individuality of each patient, understanding that each interaction shapes their experience and ultimately, their satisfaction and engagement with your practice.

Embracing a patient-first approach requires a paradigm shift at all levels of your organization. It starts with actively listening to your patients, using their feedback as a compass to guide your practice's policies, services, and improvements. It's about creating an environment where patients feel seen, heard, and respected, fostering a sense of trust and belonging. This doesn't merely extend to patient care; it influences practice operations, from the layout of your waiting room to the ease of scheduling appointments and accessing information. Every touchpoint is an opportunity to demonstrate your commitment to their well-being.

Moreover, implementing a patient-first strategy means leveraging technology and innovative practices to better serve patient needs. Telehealth, patient portals, and digital health tools are not just conveniences but necessities in modern healthcare delivery. They provide patients with greater control over their health journey, improving access and engagement. However, technology is just a tool, and its true value comes from how it's used to enhance the patient experience, not replace the human touch that is at the heart of healthcare.

A patient-first approach also necessitates a cultural shift within the practice. It involves training and motivating your team to adopt a patient-centered mindset. This might mean reevaluating your hiring practices, investing in staff training, and recognizing and rewarding behaviors that align with patient-first values. It's about building a unified team that shares the vision of delivering care that is not only clinically excellent but also compassionate and personalized. Encouraging open communication and collaboration amongst staff can further ensure that patient care is seamless and holistic.

In conclusion, adopting a patient-first approach is not just a path to enhancing patient satisfaction and engagement; it's a blueprint for practice growth and success. It challenges us to rethink how we deliver healthcare, pushing us to innovate, continuously improve, and above all, remember the core reason behind our work: the well-being of our patients. In a world where patients have more choices and higher expectations than ever before, practices that put their patients first will not only survive but thrive. Let this commitment to your patients be the compass that guides your practice into the future, defining every action and decision, and watch as it transforms not just patient outcomes, but the very essence of your healthcare practice.

Chapter 4:
Building and Retaining a High-Performance Team

In this vibrant era of healthcare, the heartbeat of a thriving medical practice is its team. To steer through the winds of change and come out ahead, it's essential to construct and nurture a team that not only meets the bar but surpasses it with agility, dedication, and excellence. Building such a team requires more than just hiring the right people; it's about inspiring every member to align with the practice's vision, engage in continuous improvement, and contribute to a culture of excellence. It's about recognizing that each individual's growth contributes to the practice's success. Therefore, laying the foundation for this high-performance team involves intentional actions: from personalized training that sharpens skills to creating a compelling work environment that fosters innovation, collaboration, and well-being. Remember, the investment in your team's growth is a direct investment in the sustainability and expansion of your practice. By embedding incentives that resonate with your staff's aspirations and facilitating a culture where excellence is the norm, you position your practice not just as a workplace, but as a launchpad for professional and personal fulfillment. This chapter will serve as your compass in cultivating such an environment, turning challenges into stepping stones for growth and transforming your medical practice into a beacon of health, excellence, and innovation.

Maintain Staff with Effective Training and Incentives

In the rapidly evolving landscape of healthcare, sustaining a high-performance team necessitates a proactive approach to staff development and motivation. A team that is well-trained and adequately rewarded is not just more efficient; it's also more engaged and committed to the vision of your medical practice. Let's dive into how effective training and incentives can become your secret weapons in building and retaining a dream team.

First off, training should never be seen as a one-time event but rather as an ongoing journey. It's crucial to invest in continuous education that keeps your staff at the forefront of medical advances and administrative efficiencies. This might mean setting aside resources for external courses, but also harnessing the power of peer-to-peer learning within your practice. Encourage your more experienced staff to mentor newer members, fostering an environment of growth and learning. This not only updates the skill set of your entire team but also boosts morale by showing your staff that you believe in their potential to evolve.

However, knowledge and skill development is only one piece of the puzzle. To truly unlock the potential of your team, pairing training with meaningful incentives is key. Incentives don't always have to be monetary; recognition, career advancement opportunities, and a say in decision-making processes can be just as motivating. The trick is to tailor these incentives to match the individual needs and aspirations of your staff members. This personal approach shows your team that their hard work is seen and valued, deeply rooting their loyalty to your practice.

Implementing a structured incentive program ensures clarity and fairness, setting clear benchmarks for performance and corresponding rewards. Whether it's through an Employee of the Month award, annual bonuses based on the practice's performance, or opportunities to attend prestigious conferences, your staff should feel a direct correlation between their efforts and the benefits they receive. This not only motivates them to maintain high performance levels but also turns them into advocates for your practice, attracting like-minded professionals to your team.

In conclusion, maintaining a dedicated and high-performing staff is less about finding the perfect people and more about nurturing the team you have. By committing to continuous training and creating a culture of recognition and reward, you can inspire your staff to grow with your practice. Remember, the strength of your medical practice lies not just in the services you provide but in the team that stands behind them. Invest in your people, and the returns will go far beyond what you initially imagined.

Creating a Culture of Growth and Excellence

In the demanding world of healthcare, where the blend of science and human compassion unfolds every day, building and nurturing a high-performance team is not just optimal; it's imperative. As medical practice owners, doctors, and nurse practitioners continue to navigate the complexities of patient care and practice management, fostering a culture that prioritizes growth and excellence becomes the linchpin to not only surviving but also thriving in this dynamic environment.

The journey towards cultivating such a culture begins with setting clear, ambitious goals that stretch the capabilities of your team, yet are achievable with concerted effort. It's about painting a big picture that resonates with everyone in your practice. Whether it's enhancing patient satisfaction, cutting down wait times, or implementing cutting-edge technology, the objectives should align with the core values of your practice, providing everyone with a north star to guide their efforts.

Communication is the bloodstream of a high-performance culture. Transparent, open lines of dialogue between all levels of staff ensure that everyone is on the same wavelength. It's not just about relaying information but also about actively listening to feedback, concerns, and suggestions. This two-way street emboldens team members to voice their ideas, fostering a sense of ownership and accountability that is crucial for growth and excellence.

Recognition and reward systems play a critical role in motivating and retaining top talent. It's essential to celebrate not just the big victories but also the small wins along the way. Acknowledging individual and team achievements reinforces positive behaviors and encourages everyone to keep aiming higher. Tailoring rewards to match the preferences of your workforce can further elevate their effectiveness, be it through professional development opportunities, financial bonuses, or public acknowledgment.

Investing in ongoing education and training is another cornerstone of a growth-oriented culture. The healthcare landscape is evolving rapidly, and staying abreast of the latest practices, technologies, and regulations is paramount. Encouraging and facilitating continuous learning demonstrates a commitment to your team's professional and personal development, which, in turn, enhances patient care and practice performance.

Empowering your team to take initiative and lead projects or improvements within the practice fosters a sense of empowerment and engagement. It's about trusting your team to make decisions and take actions that align with the practice's goals and values. This empowerment can transform the workplace atmosphere, making it more dynamic, innovative, and conducive to excellence.

Constructive feedback is another pillar of a thriving culture. Regular performance reviews, focused not on criticism but on growth and improvement, help individuals understand their strengths and areas for development. It leads to tangible action plans that align personal aspirations with the practice's objectives, creating a win-win scenario for all involved.

In the relentless pursuit of excellence, it's crucial to maintain a balance between professional demands and personal well-being. Promoting a healthy work-life balance by providing flexible working conditions, mindfulness sessions, or stress management workshops can support mental and physical health, reducing burnout and turnover.

Finally, building a culture of growth and excellence is an ongoing process, not a one-time initiative. It requires patience, persistence, and an unwavering commitment to the vision you have set for your practice. It's about celebrating the journey as much as the destination, learning from setbacks, and continuously evolving to meet the changing needs of your patients and teams.

In conclusion, as healthcare professionals, the commitment to caring for others is at the heart of what we do. By nurturing a culture that champions growth and excellence within our practice, we not only enhance our team's satisfaction and performance but also elevate the level of care we provide to our patients. It's a journey that demands our best, and together, we can achieve remarkable things.

Chapter 5:
Leveraging Healthcare Innovations

In an era where healthcare is rapidly evolving, medical practices stand at the cusp of transformation, poised to harness the power of innovation. Within this landscape, our journey pivots to embracing state-of-the-art technologies and progressive methodologies that redefine patient care and practice growth. Imagine your practice not just keeping pace but leading the charge in adopting new value-based programs that align closely with patient outcomes, thereby not just meeting but exceeding modern healthcare expectations. The investment in technology, far from being a mere expenditure, becomes the linchpin in supporting your practice's expansion, offering tools that streamline operations, enhance patient engagement, and catalyze the steady climb towards operational excellence. This chapter unfolds the blueprint for integrating these innovations into the fabric of your medical practice, encapsulating how state-of-the-art systems and forward-thinking approaches can profoundly magnify the scope and scale of your services. From electronic health records that provide instantaneous, error-free patient data to telemedicine services that bridge the gap between convenience and necessity, the arsenal of tools at your disposal is vast and ripe for the taking. Embark on this journey with a vision to not just adapt but thrive, ensuring that every stride taken is a leap towards a future where your practice is not just a healthcare provider, but a beacon of innovation and exemplary patient care.

Leverage New Value-Based Programs

The healthcare landscape is evolving rapidly, and at the heart of this transformation is a shift towards value-based programs. As medical practice owners, tapping into these programs isn't just innovative; it's essential for growth. The movement away from fee-for-service models toward value-based care is not just a trend but a profound paradigm shift that is reshaping the economics and delivery of healthcare.

Value-based programs reward healthcare providers for the quality of care they give to patients, emphasizing positive outcomes rather than the quantity of services delivered. This shift offers an unprecedented opportunity for medical practice owners to align financial incentives with patient outcomes, fostering a healthcare environment where patient well-being is paramount. Engaging in these programs requires a holistic approach to patient care, one that encompasses preventive services, efficient treatment of chronic diseases, and comprehensive management of health conditions.

The journey to integrating value-based care into your practice may seem daunting, but the rewards are multifaceted. Initially, it can set your practice apart, demonstrating a commitment to healthcare excellence and patient satisfaction. Participating in value-based programs can not only enhance your practice's reputation but can also lead to financial incentives that directly benefit your bottom line. Moreover, adopting this model encourages a team-based approach to care, which can improve job satisfaction and retention among your staff.

To leverage these new value-based programs, start by educating yourself and your team about the different available schemes and their eligibility criteria. Government resources, such as the Centers for Medicare & Medicaid Services (CMS), provide comprehensive guides and tools to help healthcare providers understand and navigate these programs. By becoming familiar with the incentives, penalties, and reporting requirements, you can make informed decisions that align with your practice's goals and strengths.

Embrace technology as your ally in this transition. Sophisticated health IT systems can streamline data collection, patient tracking, and reporting processes, essentials in demonstrating value-based care outcomes. Investing in technology that supports electronic health records (EHRs), patient engagement tools, and data analytics platforms can empower your practice to meet the rigorous performance metrics of value-based programs efficiently.

Engaging your patients in their care is another pivotal aspect of succeeding in value-based programs. Implement strategies that foster communication, education, and shared decision-making with patients. Tools like patient portals, secure messaging, telehealth, and mobile health apps can enhance patient engagement and satisfaction, leading to better outcomes and, consequently, higher reimbursement under value-based contracts.

Pilot programs and quality improvement projects within your practice can provide insights and prepare your team for broader implementation of value-based care. Start small with a focus on high-need areas that can show quick wins, such as chronic disease management or preventive care initiatives. These projects can serve as learning experiences, fostering a culture of continuous improvement and innovation among your staff.

Collaboration and partnerships with other healthcare providers and institutions can also play a vital role in thriving under value-based care. Building a network with local hospitals, specialists, and community health organizations can improve care coordination, enhance patient outcomes, and enable shared savings arrangements, further boosting the financial viability of value-based care for your practice.

Remember, transitioning to value-based programs is not just a compliance exercise; it's a strategic decision that positions your practice for sustainable growth in a rapidly changing healthcare environment. It requires commitment, flexibility, and a forward-thinking mindset that views challenges as opportunities for improvement and innovation.

Finally, let the motivation to improve patient care drive your journey towards value-based healthcare. The passion for making a tangible difference in patients' lives is the north star that should guide every strategic decision and investment. By leveraging new value-based programs, you are not just adapting to change; you are leading it, setting a benchmark for quality, efficiency, and compassion in healthcare.

Investing in Technology that Supports Practice Growth

In the rapidly evolving healthcare landscape, staying ahead isn't just about keeping pace; it's about setting the pace. As we delve into the significance of investing in technology that not only meets the demands of the present but champions the growth of your practice, it's essential to recognize technology as an ally in your journey towards expansion and excellence. This section explores how strategic technological investments can be a game-changer for medical practices seeking sustainable growth.

First, consider the digital transformation sweeping across healthcare. Electronic Health Records (EHRs) have replaced outdated filing systems, telemedicine is bridging the gap between providers and patients separated by distance, and AI-driven diagnostics tools are offering insights with precision that was once thought impossible. These advancements are not just bells and whistles but pivotal tools that can drive patient engagement, streamline operations, and enhance the quality of care provided.

The journey begins with understanding your practice's unique needs and goals. Are you looking to improve patient satisfaction? Increase operational efficiency? Or maybe, enhance your diagnostic capabilities? The technology you choose to invest in should directly support these objectives, enabling your practice to not only meet but exceed its goals.

Implementing an EHR system, for instance, can drastically reduce administrative burdens, allowing your staff to focus more on patient care than paperwork. But investing in technology goes beyond mere acquisition. It entails fostering a culture of adaptability where your team is not just comfortable but proficient in leveraging these tools. This might involve regular training sessions or bringing in experts to ensure a smooth transition and integration into your daily operations.

Equally important is prioritizing data security. With cyber-attacks on the rise, protecting patient information is paramount. Investing in secure, compliant technologies will not only safeguard your practice against data breaches but also build patient trust—a crucial component of practice growth.

Telemedicine, once a novelty, has now become a necessity. Its rapid adoption amidst global health challenges has proven its value in providing continuous care while maximizing practice efficiency. The convenience and accessibility it offers patients are undeniable. However, its implementation should be approached judiciously, ensuring it complements your practice's services rather than complicates them.

Moreover, AI and machine learning are offering unprecedented opportunities for diagnostic accuracy, personalized treatment plans, and predictive analytics. These technologies can transform how care is delivered, making early detection and prevention a more tangible reality for practices of all sizes. The key is identifying the right tools that align with your practice's vision and patient needs.

But let's not forget, at the heart of all this technology are the people it serves. Any technological investment should enhance the patient-provider relationship, not distance it. Tools that facilitate better communication, streamline appointment scheduling, and offer more accessible health information empower patients to be active participants in their health journey, leading to better outcomes and higher satisfaction rates.

In conclusion, investing in technology is not merely about keeping up with the trends. It's about strategically choosing tools that will propel your practice towards its growth objectives while enhancing the quality of care. It's a thoughtful process of selection, implementation, and adaptation that, when done right, can yield significant dividends for your practice and your patients.

As you navigate this journey, remember that the path to technological integration is continuous. It requires an ongoing commitment to evaluation, adaptation, and education. But with the right mindset and strategic approach, the investment in technology can be a powerful catalyst for growth, setting your practice apart as a leader in the healthcare innovations landscape.

Chapter 6:
Financial and Operational Excellence

In the complex and ever-evolving landscape of healthcare, understanding the nuances of financial and operational excellence can seem daunting, yet it's undeniably critical for your practice's sustained growth and success. It's here in this nexus of your medical practice that the true potential for transformative change lies. Picture your practice not just surviving, but thriving, moving seamlessly from good to great. This transformation begins with mastering the dual pillars of financial health and operational efficiency. Financial acumen paired with operational expertise creates a synergy that propels your practice forward, ensuring that every aspect of your business is performing at its peak.

Imagine a scenario where your billing processes are not just adequate, but optimized, capturing every opportunity for revenue without compromising on patient care. This level of precision in financial management is attainable and starts with making sure you're billing correctly and efficiently. It's an element that directly impacts your bottom line and patient satisfaction, offering a clear path to financial stability.

On the operational side, consider the power of streamlined practice operations, where every process is refined for maximum efficiency. It's about identifying bottlenecks before they become roadblocks and leveraging insights to make smart, timely decisions. An efficiently run practice not only boosts your team's morale but also enhances patient experiences, creating a ripple effect of positive outcomes across your business.

To achieve excellence in these areas, you'll need to foster an environment of continuous improvement and embrace strategies that support growth. This means adopting a proactive mindset that anticipates needs and adapts solutions in real-time, ensuring your practice is always one step ahead. It's about becoming a vigilant guardian of your practice's resources, optimizing every aspect of your operations to unlock new avenues for growth and stability.

So as you chart your course towards financial and operational excellence, remember that the path is not just about overcoming challenges, but about seizing opportunities. It's a journey that requires dedication, insight, and an unwavering commitment to excellence, but the rewards—a thriving practice and the highest level of patient care—are within your reach. Let this chapter be your guide to refining your practice's operations and financial strategies, setting a new standard of excellence that propels you towards your goals.

Make Sure You Are Billing Correctly

In the heart of financial and operational excellence lies a pillar so crucial, yet so fraught with pitfalls: correct billing. As medical practitioners, our primary mission is healing and bringing solace to our patients. Yet, we can't shy away from the fact that our practices are also businesses, which means revenue management is just as critical. Let's dive into how we can ensure our billing process isn't just a routine task, but a cornerstone of our practice's success.

The first step towards mastering billing is understanding the complexities of coding and insurance policies. Each procedure, each diagnosis, comes with its unique code and, sometimes, a plethora of sub-codes. It's imperative that you and your staff are not just familiar with these, but that you're experts. Errors in this area are not just common; they are costly. They can lead to claims being denied, payments being delayed, and in some cases, audits by insurance companies or regulatory bodies.

Invest in training for yourself and your team. I can't stress this enough. Knowledge is power, more so in the world of medical billing. Regular workshops, webinars, and courses should be on your calendar. The landscape of insurance policies and medical coding is ever-evolving, and staying updated is not optional; it's mandatory.

Integrating the right technology can bridge many gaps in the billing process. There are several state-of-the-art medical billing software systems designed to reduce errors, streamline the billing process, and ensure compliance with the latest regulations. They can automatically update codes, flag potential errors before submission, and even follow up on pending claims. It's an investment that pays for itself in spades.

Don't overlook the importance of clear communication with patients regarding their bills. Confusion and misunderstandings can lead to disputes, delays in payment, and, most devastatingly, erosion of trust between patient and provider. Ensure your billing statements are patient-friendly. Break down charges clearly, offer multiple payment options, and always have someone knowledgeable available to answer questions and resolve issues promptly.

Perform regular audits of your billing process. It's like a routine health check-up but for your practice's financial health. This involves reviewing policies, reconciling payments with services provided, and ensuring compliance with insurance and regulatory requirements. It can help identify patterns of errors or inefficiencies that, once addressed, can significantly increase your revenue.

Collaboration with insurance companies is also key. Building a positive, proactive relationship with these entities can help solve issues more rapidly and keep the claims process smooth. Understand their policies, stay informed about any changes, and don't hesitate to reach out for clarifications or to challenge unjust denials. Yes, it takes time, but it's worth it.

One overlooked aspect of billing is training patients to understand their responsibilities. This means clear communication about co-pays, deductibles, and what their insurance covers. Patients who understand their bills are less likely to be surprised by them and more likely to pay on time. Educating patients is as crucial as treating them.

Lastly, always remember the power of empathy. A billing error or an unexpected bill can cause significant stress for patients. Approach these situations with understanding and a willingness to find solutions. Your role as a healer extends into every aspect of your practice, billing included.

In conclusion, billing correctly isn't just about reducing errors or increasing revenue; it's about integrity, efficiency, and respect for your patients. It's a reflection of your commitment to not only their health but also to the health of your practice. By focusing on accuracy, compliance, technology, and empathy, you set up your practice for financial success and operational excellence. Turn the challenge of billing into your practice's strength, and watch as your business, and more importantly, your patients, thrive.

Optimizing Practice Operations for Efficiency

Transforming the operations of your practice for peak efficiency isn't just about cutting costs; it's about smartly reallocating resources where they can make the most impact. Think of it as trimming the sails of a boat for smoother sailing, rather than simply throwing cargo overboard. It involves a critical look at your practice's workflow, identifying bottlenecks, and implementing solutions that allow everyone in your team to work at their highest potential. By doing so, you set up a virtuous cycle of improvement where efficiency breeds more time, and more time breeds opportunities for growth and enhancement of patient care.

One of the first steps to optimizing operations is embracing technology. From electronic health records

(EHRs) to online appointment scheduling, the right tech tools can do wonders to ease the administrative load on your staff. However, it's crucial to choose solutions that integrate well with your existing systems and processes. A piecemeal approach where systems do not communicate with each other only leads to further inefficiency. Therefore, carefully evaluate technology that not only solves immediate problems but also scales with your practice's growth.

Process review is another essential aspect of achieving operational excellence. It involves dissecting each procedure your practice carries out, from patient check-in to follow-up care. Where are the redundancies? Where do patients or staff members get frustrated? By identifying these pain points, you can begin to redesign your workflows in a way that's both more satisfying for your patients and more efficient for your team. Remember, small changes can have ripple effects, significantly enhancing overall efficiency.

Effective communication within your practice cannot be overstated in its importance. Clarity in roles, responsibilities, and expectations eliminates confusion and enables your team to work like a well-oiled machine. Consider implementing regular briefings where staff can discuss the day's schedule, share concerns, and brainstorm solutions to ongoing challenges. Such meetings can foster a sense of teamwork and uncover innovative ideas for improving practice operations that you might not have considered.

In the journey to operational excellence, remember that improvement is a continuous process, not a destination. Be prepared to iteratively assess and adjust your strategies. Encourage feedback from your staff and patients alike, as this will provide invaluable insights into where further optimizations can be made. With a commitment to efficiency, not only can you improve your bottom line, but you can also enhance patient care, reduce burnout among your team, and position your practice for sustainable growth in an ever-evolving healthcare landscape.

Chapter 7:
Developing Strategic Partnerships

In the evolving landscape of healthcare, forging strategic partnerships stands out as a transformative strategy to unlock growth and innovation for medical practices. The power of collaboration cannot be overstated; when medical practices join forces with the right partners, they create synergies that can lead to expanded services, improved patient care, and operational efficiencies. This chapter zeroes in on the actionable steps to identify, approach, and cultivate such partnerships that align with your practice's goals and values. Whether it's partnering with cutting-edge healthcare technology vendors who are as committed to your success as their own or initiating collaboration with other healthcare providers to offer a more comprehensive care continuum, the focus here is on creating win-win scenarios. These partnerships not only help in scaling your practice but also ensure that you remain at the forefront of high-quality patient care. Through strategic alliances, you're not just growing your practice; you're elevating the healthcare experience for your patients and setting a new standard in the industry. It's about moving beyond the conventional boundaries of medical practice to embrace a future where collaboration and innovation lead to unprecedented growth and success.

Work with Vendors Who Want to Truly Partner and Not Just Sell You a Solution

In the dynamic world of healthcare, forming strategic alliances with vendors is more than a matter of convenience—it's a strategic imperative. However, it's vital to choose partners who are as deeply invested in your success as you are. These are vendors who look beyond the transactional nature of business to forge relationships grounded in mutual growth, understanding, and respect. They don't just want to sell you a product or service; they aim to be an integral part of your journey to excellence.

Identifying these partner-oriented vendors begins with a keen understanding of your medical practice's unique needs and future aspirations. It's about finding those who are willing to listen and adapt their solutions to fit your evolving requirements. A true vendor partner is one that takes the time to understand the intricacies of your operations and challenges. They are ready to innovate and co-create solutions that not only solve present problems but also anticipate future needs, ensuring your practice remains at the forefront of healthcare excellence.

Engaging with the right vendor partners necessitates thorough vetting. It involves delving into their track record of customer support, innovation, and flexibility. Do they have a history of listening to and acting on client feedback? Are they known for their commitment to their clients' growth, not just their own? These are critical questions that require candid answers. Moreover, the best partnerships are built on transparent communication. This means regular check-ins, honest feedback loops, and a shared vision for what success looks like.

Once the right vendor partners are identified, nurturing these relationships becomes paramount. This goes beyond the occasional business review or transaction. It's about continuous engagement, sharing insights, challenges, and achievements. It includes opening lines of communication for feedback and innovation, creating a symbiotic relationship where both parties are invested in finding ways to enhance outcomes. Your vendor partners should be thought of as an extension of your team—a source of expertise, support, and innovation.

In conclusion, choosing to work with vendors who seek a genuine partnership can significantly influence the trajectory of your medical practice's growth. These relationships transcend mere transactions, embodying a shared commitment to excellence, innovation, and mutual success. By carefully selecting and nurturing these strategic alliances, you position your practice not just for growth, but for a sustainable transformation that benefits your patients, your team, and the broader healthcare landscape.

Collaborating with Other Healthcare Providers for Mutual Growth

In an era where the healthcare landscape is continually evolving, forging strategic partnerships with other healthcare providers isn't just beneficial; it's essential for mutual growth. Collaboration can take many forms, from referrals and shared resources to joint ventures in providing comprehensive care. This synergy not only amplifies your practice's capabilities but also offers a holistic approach to patient care, ultimately enhancing your reputation and patient base.

Initiating a collaboration begins with identifying potential partners who share your commitment to quality care and growth. Look beyond the confines of traditional healthcare settings and consider how aligning with specialists, community health organizations, and even wellness centers might offer your patients a spectrum of services that a single practice simply can't provide alone. The key here is to seek partners whose strengths complement your weaknesses and vice versa, creating a scenario where the sum is indeed greater than its parts.

Once potential partners are identified, transparency and clear communication are paramount. Establish mutual goals and understand each other's expectations and limitations. Drafting a formal agreement can help solidify this understanding, outlining the details of resource sharing, financial arrangements, and how to jointly handle patient care. This step ensures that everyone is on the same page and aims to minimize conflicts that might arise.

With the logistics in place, leveraging technology can facilitate seamless collaboration. Investing in interoperable electronic health records (EHRs) allows for the efficient sharing of patient information, making coordinated care more practical and effective. Moreover, technology can aid in tracking the outcomes of your collaborative efforts, providing tangible data to gauge the success of the partnership and identify areas for improvement.

Ultimately, the goal of collaborating with other healthcare providers is to foster a network that supports not just the growth of your practice, but also the well-being of your patients. By joining forces with like-minded partners, you're poised to deliver a level of care that's greater than what you could achieve independently, driving the industry forward. Remember, in this journey of growth and improvement, you're not alone. Through strategic partnerships, the potential for success and impact is boundless.

Chapter 8:
Sustaining Growth and
Preventing Burnout

The journey through the chapters of this book has equipped you with the knowledge and strategies necessary to propel your medical practice into a realm of sustainable growth and improvement. Yet, it's crucial to remember that the endurance of this growth lies in the balance between pushing for continuous advancement and guarding against the creeping specter of burnout. Sustaining growth in your medical practice isn't just about the numbers or the scale of operations; it's profoundly about nurturing an environment where both the practice and its people can thrive.

In the relentless pursuit of excellence, it's easy to overlook the necessity of resilience and self-care. Preventing burnout is not a sidebar to your growth strategy; it is intrinsic to it. The well-being of your team is paramount. A burnt-out team is disengaged, less productive, and, ultimately, detrimental to the patient experience. This is why embedding practices that promote well-being, encourage open communication, and foster a supportive work environment is critical. It's about creating a culture where your team members can openly discuss their challenges without fear of reprimand, where they feel valued and heard.

Moreover, the commitment to personal growth and development should mirror the commitment to the growth of the practice. Encouraging your team to set personal goals, pursue continued education, and engage in professional development opportunities not only combats stagnation but also infuses your practice with fresh ideas and perspectives. It's a symbiotic relationship; as your team grows, so does the capacity of your practice to innovate and excel. Leverage this by investing in people-centric practices that underscore the value of every team member's contribution to the overarching mission.

But let's not forget about you, the leader at the helm of this endeavor. Sustaining growth necessitates that you, too, must be vigilant against burnout. Leadership demands resilience, and resilience is fortified by mindfulness, rest, and a supportive network. It's imperative to set boundaries, seek mentorship, and engage in self-reflection to maintain clarity and purpose. Your leadership style sets the tone for the entire organization. A leader who models balance, open communication, and self-care empowers their team to adopt these practices.

Finally, as you move forward, carrying the insights and strategies from this book, remember that growth is a journey, not a destination. There will be challenges, setbacks, and victories. However, the true measure of success lies in the ability to sustain progress and nurture an environment where both the practice and its people can flourish. Your dedication to preventing burnout and promoting well-being is the cornerstone of not just surviving in the healthcare landscape but thriving. Embrace this mission, and watch as your practice transforms into a beacon of sustained growth and excellence.

Appendix A:
Appendix

In stepping beyond the final chapter of this guide, you've shown not just a commitment to the growth of your medical practice, but a readiness to elevate every aspect of your operations, patient care, and team development. The journey towards amplifying your practice is an ongoing process, ripe with continual learning, adaptation, and the seizing of new opportunities. That's where this Appendix comes into play.

Resources for Medical Practice Owners

Navigating the complex world of healthcare requires a solid base of resources. Whether it's staying informed on the latest healthcare innovations, understanding regulatory changes, or simply finding inspiration for your team, knowing where to look is half the battle. We've curated a collection of invaluable resources including professional healthcare associations, cutting-edge research publications, and online forums full of peer support. These are aimed at keeping you at the forefront of medical practice management, helping you to not just keep pace with industry standards but to set them.

Make a habit of engaging with these resources regularly. Subscribe to newsletters, participate in forum discussions, and perhaps most importantly, make connections with your peers. The collective wisdom of a community can provide insights and solutions that you might not have considered.

Checklist for Implementing Growth Strategies

Change isn't easy, and even the most well-intentioned plans can go astray if they're not followed through with diligence and regular reassessment. To assist in the practical application of the strategies discussed in this book, we've included a comprehensive checklist. This tool is designed to help you systematically implement changes within your practice, ensuring that no aspect of your growth plan is overlooked.

- **Assess Your Current Practice Landscape:** Conduct a thorough review of your practice's strengths, weaknesses, opportunities, and threats (SWOT analysis).

- **Identify Revenue Leakages:** Utilize analytics and audit trails to pinpoint where you might be losing revenue and take corrective action.

- **Enhance Patient Engagement:** Develop a plan to implement or improve remote communication channels and other patient engagement strategies.

- **Retain and Train Your Team:** Create a detailed plan for staff development, including training programs and incentives to boost retention.

- **Leverage Healthcare Innovations:** Identify at least one new technology or value-based program to implement in the next quarter.

- **Optimize Operational Efficiency:** Review your current operational workflows and identify areas for improvement.

- **Develop Strategic Partnerships:** Make a list of potential partners, outlining what you seek in a partnership and what you can offer.

This checklist serves as a roadmap, but it's essential to tailor its application to your practice's unique needs and circumstances. Regularly revisit and adjust your strategies in response to both the successes and challenges you encounter along the way.

In embarking on this journey of growth, remember, it's not just about expanding your practice but enriching the quality of care you provide and the work environment you create for your team. The path ahead is as rewarding as it is challenging, filled with opportunities to learn, adapt, and thrive. Your dedication to embracing change and leading your practice toward a brighter future is the most potent catalyst for growth there is.

Let this Appendix serve as both a springboard and a guide as you navigate the complexities of healthcare management, inspiring continuous improvement and innovation within your practice. The impact you make in the lives of your patients and staff is invaluable, and with each step forward, you're creating a legacy of excellence in healthcare.

Resources for Medical Practice Owners

The journey of medical practice ownership is laden with challenges, opportunities, and the constant drive to improve both patient care and business aspects. As we venture deeper into this era of healthcare, the need for resources that can guide, inspire, and assist in making informed decisions is more critical than ever. Whether you're looking to enhance patient satisfaction, leverage healthcare innovations, or ensure operational excellence, these resources are tailored to foster growth and sustainability in your medical practice.

- **Professional Development Workshops and Webinars:** Continuing education isn't just about maintaining licensure—it's a powerful tool for practice growth. Seek out workshops and webinars that focus on emerging healthcare trends, management strategies, and technological advancements. Engaging in these educational forums can provide you with fresh insights and actionable steps to take your practice to the next level. Remember, a thriving practice is one that evolves with the times and adapts to new challenges ahead.

- **Healthcare Business Consultants:** Sometimes, an external perspective can unveil opportunities and efficiencies that aren't immediately apparent from the inside. Healthcare business consultants specialize in dissecting the workings of medical practices to identify areas of improvement, strategize on revenue enhancement, and streamline operations. Investing in a consultant might seem like a significant step, but it's one that can lead to substantial returns by optimizing your practice's performance.

- **Networking Groups and Forums:** There's immense value in learning from peers and sharing experiences with fellow medical practice owners. Networking groups and online forums serve as a platform to exchange ideas, challenges, solutions, and strategies. These communities can be particularly beneficial for uncovering real-world advice and support, providing not just professional connection, but also moral support from individuals who understand the unique pressures of running a medical practice.

In your pursuit of growth and excellence, remember that the resources at your disposal are numerous, but selecting those that align with your practice's goals and values is key. Embrace every opportunity to learn, adapt, and innovate. After all, the path to success in medical practice ownership isn't just about navigating challenges—it's about seizing opportunities for transformation and growth.

Checklist for Implementing Growth Strategies

Growth isn't just a goal; it's a journey that requires meticulous planning, unwavering dedication, and an unshakable belief in your practice's mission. As you pivot towards expanding your reach and enhancing the services of your medical practice, consider this checklist as your roadmap. It's designed to facilitate not just growth but sustainable success, ensuring that every step you take aligns with the core values and objectives of your practice.

- **Set Clear, Measurable Objectives:** What does growth mean for your practice? Is it expanding your patient base, introducing new services, or perhaps enhancing operational efficiency? Define clear, attainable goals and set a timeline for achieving them. Remember, growth should be quantifiable. Whether it's a 20% increase in patient enrollment or reducing patient wait times by 15 minutes, having specific targets will keep your team focused and motivated.

- **Engage and Empower Your Team:** The heart of your practice beats because of the people who work tirelessly behind the scenes. Engaging your staff in your growth plans isn't just beneficial; it's essential. Create an environment that encourages feedback, fosters professional development, and recognizes exceptional contributions. When your team feels valued and part of the practice's success story, their commitment to achieving collective goals multiplies exponentially.

- **Analyze and Adapt to Patient Needs:** In the rapidly evolving world of healthcare, the needs and expectations of patients change continually. Stay ahead by regularly gathering patient feedback through surveys, suggestion boxes, or informal conversations. Use this invaluable insight to adapt your services, ensuring they meet or exceed patient expectations. Remember, a satisfied patient is not just a loyal patron but also a walking, talking billboard for your practice.

Implementing growth strategies requires a balance of ambition and realism. It's about pushing boundaries while staying grounded in the practicalities of day-to-day operations. It requires a team that's not just skilled but also passionate about making a difference in patients' lives. And most importantly, it necessitates a leader who can steer the ship with a steady hand, guiding the practice through both calm and turbulent waters towards the horizon of success. Your journey of growth starts now. Embrace it with open arms, a clear vision, and a determination to succeed.

About the Author

Theo Harvey, MS, MBA is the CEO and Co-Founder of SynsorMed, a digital healthcare company transforming virtual care. Prior to SynsorMed, he advised many hospitals, healthcare systems, and small practices on how technology can transform their current workflows, lower the cost of healthcare delivery, and increase patient engagement. His company is backed by Google.

In addition, Mr. Harvey has served as an Adjunct professor for Healthcare Informatics at the Georgia State University, and held several Business Development roles within Cisco where he managed large accounts like the Veteran's Administration, AT&T, Sprint, and British Telecom. He received his MBA from Emory University and Masters of Electrical Engineering from Georgia Institute of Technology. He currently lives in Tampa, Florida with his wife Naja and two children Laila and Langston.

www.ingramcontent.com/pod-product-compliance
Lightning Source LLC
Chambersburg PA
CBHW021341160726